A Gathering of Larks

A Gathering of Larks

Letters to Saint Francis from a Modern-Day Pilgrim

ABIGAIL CARROLL

WILLIAM B. EERDMANS PUBLISHING COMPANY
GRAND RAPIDS, MICHIGAN

Wm. B. Eerdmans Publishing Co.
2140 Oak Industrial Drive N.E., Grand Rapids, Michigan 49505
www.eerdmans.com

© 2017 Abigail Carroll
All rights reserved
Published 2017
Printed in the United States of America

22 21 20 19 18 17   1 2 3 4 5 6 7

ISBN 978-0-8028-7445-0

Library of Congress Cataloging-in-Publication Data

A catalog record for this book is available from the Library of Congress

The birds depicted in *A Gathering of Larks* are reproduced from John James Audubon's *Birds of America*. Printed between 1827 and 1838, *Birds of America* contains 435 life-sized watercolors of North American birds, all reproduced from hand-engraved plates. The images reproduced here are provided courtesy of the John James Audubon Center at Mill Grove in Audubon, Pennsylvania, and the Montgomery County Audubon Collection.

Dedication

For my fellow modern-day pilgrims
Jennifer Decker, Deborah Dickerson,
Kevin Fitton, Leigh Harder, and Manisha Munshi,
whose keen, encouraging feedback has strengthened
this book and whose gift of friendship
has gladdened my journey.

Contents

Introduction

A letter bridges distance. It travels roads, crosses borders, and traverses mountain ranges and oceans, carrying the words—and a bit of the heart—of the letter-writer. The letters in this book also bridge distance, but of a different kind. They travel across time, reaching out to a figure whose life was framed by cobblestone streets, feudalism, lepers' bells, troubadours, woolen tunics, wood smoke, minstrels' lutes, and crusaders' swords. Francesco Bernardone, the man who would become famous as Saint Francis of Assisi, inhabited a wholly different world than the one we live in, and yet the echo of his fascinating, at times beguiling, twelfth-century life reverberates through the centuries and speaks to us today.

While many people feel an affinity for Francis all these centuries later, a thick shroud of romanticism threatens to replace the man with the myth. For most of my life, the St. Francis I have encountered has been as garden statuary, prayer card images, children's book illustrations, and stained-glass windows. In these letters, I attempt to bridge the distance between who Francesco Bernardone really was and who we have made him to be. Each letter is an invitation bidding the life of this holy man from Assisi to speak for itself. Together, they probe his humanness, poke fun at the sentimentality surrounding his persona, and attempt to parse man and saint—getting under his halo, so to speak. If these letters manage to do that, as I hope they do, the point is less to challenge than to inquire. This is not the correspondence of an adversary or a cynic, but of one who is reverently, if candidly, curious—a modern-day pilgrim in search of a friend with whom to share the journey.

A friend rejoices with you when you rejoice, weeps with you when you mourn, and cares to know what is on your heart and mind. Likewise, I have cared to know what was on Francesco's heart and mind when he wandered the fields of Umbria, kissed a leper, heard a crucifix speak, stole from his father to restore a crumbling church, parted with his clothes in the public square, walked to Rome barefoot, scissored Clare's locks with a tender hand, attempted to single-handedly halt the Fifth Crusade, tamed a ferocious wolf, underwent failed surgery on his eyes, received the stigmata on Mount Alverna, penned poems and songs that we still sing today, and died lying naked on the dusty Umbrian earth.

In these letters, I explore the spiritual landscape of Francis's life, and, as with a close friend, I invite him into the spiritual landscape of mine. By sharing with Francis my joys, hopes, questions, and doubts, these letters bridge yet another distance: the vast canyon between the head and the heart. The Swedish diplomat Dag Hammarskjöld famously said, "The longest journey of any person is the journey inward." How do we embark on that journey? Prayer and contemplation come to mind—study and reflection as well. Indeed, all manner of spiritual disciplines may help. But a simple conversation with a fellow pilgrim is often all the encouragement we need to set out on that journey, or to invigorate our step. I am thankful for those fellow pilgrims, like Francis, who have gone ahead of me and whose storied lives inspire my faith.

Prologue: The Life of Saint Francis

Francesco Bernardone was born to a wealthy Italian cloth merchant in Assisi in 1181 or 1182. His mother, Pica, baptized him John while his father was away acquiring fabrics in France, but upon returning, his father changed the name to Francesco, a choice that expressed the cultural and business promise of France in their lives. The new name would suit the young Italian well, but for reasons other than his father's, as Francesco took up the life of a French troubadour—singing, reciting poetry, drinking, and making merry. His friends dubbed him "King of the Revels," and wherever he went, he was the life of the party. When he spent a year in a Perugian dungeon as a prisoner of war and became chronically ill, fellow prisoners remarked that his sense of humor remained strong and helped buoy others' spirits.

While Francis was a natural businessman and would have succeeded in the cloth trade, he chose instead to pursue the glories of knighthood and, with his family's blessing and a fine suit of armor, set off to join the Fourth Crusade. However, a powerful but enigmatic dream his first night on the road put a halt to his plans. In the dream, a voice summoned Francis to return to Assisi, and, when he did, he suffered the humiliation of being seen as a coward. Unable to focus, he wandered the countryside. He also visited Rome at this time, though whether as pilgrim or sightseer is uncertain. At the Vatican, he was so appalled by the pittance that visitors were throwing on Saint Peter's tomb that he reached deep into his purse and flung a lavish number of coins through the confessio grate, the sound of which caught the attention of many astonished bystanders.

Both in Rome and Assisi, Francis gave liberally (some would say recklessly) to the poor, but he deeply loathed lepers—their deformities, their stench, their rags. One day when he unexpectedly encountered a leper on a long walk in the plains below Assisi, something inside Francesco changed. Instead of running away, he impetuously approached the outcast and embraced him—some say he kissed him. A new spiritual hunger had been growing in this wealthy cloth merchant's son, and on the country road that day, he found himself confronted with a challenge more personally trying than battle: to love the leper as the gospel commanded. The encounter filled Francis with a deep and surprising joy, and it helped set a new course for his life.

During his soul-searching, Francesco discovered in the countryside the ruins of a church, where he began going to pray. One day while in prayer, he heard a voice speak to him from the crucifix asking him to repair the church, which Francis took quite literally. He gave the priest a large sum of money to ensure that the candle on the altar in front would never go out. Without his father's permission, he also sold numerous bolts of fabric to raise the money for the restoration. When his father found out, he was so outraged that Francis, who had essentially stolen the goods, was forced to go into hiding. A month later, the do-good thief came out of hiding to repent and return the money in a public hearing overseen by the bishop—but with a twist. Instead of simply handing back the money, Francesco also took off his clothes and shoes and handed them to his father too. No longer was Pietro Bernardone his father; now, Francis proclaimed, God alone was his father. Leaving his family and the townspeople speechless, Francis walked away naked and singing.

Begging for bread and stones, Francis devoted himself to caring for the lepers and rebuilding the church. He also preached in the streets—sometimes in song—and appropriately called himself God's Fool (in French, *Jongleur de Dieu*). Many thought he was mad, but some were compelled by his example, and a few renounced their lives of wealth and prestige to join him. Before long they were a community, but as word got out about their extreme poverty, they fell into danger of being labeled by the church as heretics. To protect their way of life, they sought the favor of the pope, and Francis led a contingent of barefoot brothers to Rome, where they succeeded in gaining official recognition.

The community expanded in an unexpected way when sixteen-year-old Clare di Offreduccio, the aristocratic daughter of a knight, found herself deeply moved by Francis's preaching and began to meet with him and some friars to seek direction for her life. Under a great deal of pressure to marry, especially after inheriting sizeable wealth upon her father's death, she decided instead to follow what she believed was God's calling and embrace the gospel Francis's way. To her family's shock, she gave her entire inheritance away to the poor. On Palm Sunday of her eighteenth year, she dressed in her finest gown, escaped her home by cover of night, met Francis and the friars at the church, and said her vows by torchlight. As a sign of her commitment, she exchanged her dress for a habit and allowed Francis to cut off her long hair. To avoid the wrath of her angry uncles who were hot on her trail, she then fled, escorted by Francis and some friars, to a convent where she would be protected. After the storm passed, Clare and those women who soon began to join her lived as a sister community to Francis and his followers.

Francis loved nature from his youth and had a special way with animals. When people refused to listen to his teachings, he famously preached to the birds. He had a particular fondness for larks, whose color he chose to imitate with his brown frock, and during the closing years of his life a crow proved a loyal friend. One Christmas, as a way to retell the story of the Christ child's birth, Francis creatively organized a living crèche with townspeople and animals in the hilltop village of Greccio. Legend holds that while visiting the town of Gubbio, Francis learned that a wolf had been terrorizing the population and had taken the lives of several inhabitants and their livestock. Addressing the creature as Friar Wolf, he asked it to pledge peace in exchange for food. From that point on the townsfolk fed the wolf, and it no longer caused them harm. In 1872, renovators of Gubbio's *San Francesco del Pace* discovered a wolf skeleton buried under the chapel.

Francis now took his mission of reconciliation to a higher level, attempting not only to make peace between a wolf and a town, but between warring nations. Deeply saddened by the violence of the Fifth Crusade, Francis traveled barefoot to Egypt in 1219 and, at great risk to his life, attempted to end the warfare by crossing enemy lines, gaining a personal audience with the sultan Al-Kamil, and sharing his faith with him. Though the sultan did not convert to Christianity (nor, for that matter, Francis to Islam), the encounter touched both of them, and peace seemed a greater possibility. Shortly after the encounter, Al-Kamil proposed a truce, but the Crusaders refused to discuss peace, and Francis's efforts to halt the bloodshed failed.

In his later years, Francis found himself torn between the burdens of overseeing a now international brotherhood of friars (some of whom held definitions of poverty at odds with his own) and spending time in solitude and prayer. During an extended retreat alone on Mount Alverna, he experienced a powerful vision of the crucifix flanked by seraphs, and he came down from the mountain bearing the marks of Christ's wounds in his flesh, a personal partaking of his savior's suffering that he chose to guard as a private grace rather than share as a public sign. Around this time, he became almost fully blind, and sunlight hurt his constantly inflamed and watering eyes. Only half-willingly did he undergo a procedure to restore his sight through a painful cauterization of his temples. The procedure did not succeed.

Suffering from chronic illness (likely tuberculosis possibly complicated by leprosy), Francis focused his efforts on writing poems and songs, his most famous being "Canticle of the Sun," which offers praise to God for Brother Sun, Sister Moon, Brothers Wind and Air, Sister Water, Brother Fire, and Mother Earth. When a public dispute arose between two prominent figures in Assisi, both of whom were his lifelong friends, Francis added the verse "Be praised, O Lord, through those who pardon for thy love" and sent a friar to sing the canticle to the two angered men, who, moved by the lyrics, found themselves each compelled to forgive the other. It was one of Francis's final acts.

Francis died in 1226 at the age of forty-five. Before burying him, the brothers removed his clothes and placed him naked on the ground for the time it takes a man to walk a mile—as Francis had requested. It was just after sunset on an early October evening, and those who stood watch at his passing remarked that larks gathered in the skies.

The Letters

Dear Francis,

The showerhead is broken.

I've been bucketing water from the faucet,
        ladling it over my shoulders
and hair,

letting it run down my back.

This is how so many
        have done it before
and somewhere in the world even now—

a slow, monk-like cupping
        and pouring.

There is something about the breaking

and re-breaking of water
        over the arc of the body—

with each downflow,

        a baptism.

Rechristened

Dear Brother Francis,

Time to plant, time to press my nails
in dirt,
       resurrect the earth with chives,

Swiss chard, basil, beans. The shed

is dark, winter still stuck in its shingles
and boards,
       trowels, gloves, watering cans,

pots. Francis, I am learning to have faith

in seeds. Every year, I drop the grains
too close,
       thinking only a few will stem

and leaf. I do not trust the package notes,

I do not space punctilious rows or calculate
their depths.
       It seems to me no life can rise

from dust—and yet it does: year after year

this plot turns a weedy, flowering jungle
of green.
       What if the whole of a life (yours,

say, or mine) is simply this—a tiny germ

of wheat sleeping in a bed of soil?
The crop
            this shell will one day yield it will

never actually see. All it can do is dream.

A Green Thumb

Dear Francesco,

I wonder what your horse thought that day
you wandered the fields like a prince seeking

a kingdom—lost

among salvia and wild fennel, ox-eye daisies,
sunchokes, milkwort, yellow broom—

then gripped the reins

at the sight of an ash-streaked heap of rags
standing in the road, the jangle of a cow bell

at the end of a stick.

I wonder who first saw who—or did he avert
your gaze? They say you kissed that greasy

knob-fingered man

awash with sores, rank as a battlefield strewn
with death. They say, Francis, you kissed illness

itself—

afterward were never quite the same. You leapt
off the gleaming brown back of your horse

like Peter from the boat

and swam through the gentian and wind-bent
grass to commit the ludicrous deed. Tell me,

did you see in him

the leper-Christ? Did you feel his scaly skin?
Did yarrow and poppies swoosh and bend

as you galloped on?

With highest regard,

Dear Friar Minor,

For years I wore nothing
but brown,

the color of coffee, nail rust,
        bark.
It was hardly a choice,

this half-liturgical code—
        more like
a mood.

Unlike you, I did not
        wear a hood

nor, for that matter, a cord.
        Still,
wood thrush, walnut, loam—

this was my habit of sorts.

Why not blue or cream
        or charcoal gray?

I cannot say. I only know
        I wished

to feel the earth. (If I could,

I would have donned
        a lark-brown frock.)

So much for plain clothes—

Since then,
        this world has robed me
in salmon

and aqua
            and rose.

Your sister minor

Dear Francis, Patron Saint of Gardens and Lawns,

Among begonias and bleeding hearts
        in suburban backyards, you hold out rain-filled
        bowls

on the rims of which perch cardinals,
        jays, sparrows, finches, robins, wrens. They dip
        and roll

their thin-boned wings, fluff plumage
        in tiny bursts of pride, send droplets through
        the air

like shining bits of glass. Patient
        as a saint, you stay perfectly still. In fact,
        you never

actually move, which is why
        they consider you their friend. You preside over
        lawn grass

and mulch, lilies and hostas and vetch,
        patios and hammocks and winding slate paths,
        gazing balls

and lantern gnomes. I imagine you have seen
        a few pink flamingos in your life, not to mention
        pinwheels

and Christmas lights. You happily
        make room for blue-robed Madonnas in bathtub
        shrines

and praying cherubs hidden among
        the ferns. As for your form, you come in resin
        and stone,

cast concrete, even bronze.
        You're frost-proof and color-fast, your sculpted
        tunic unruffled

by the breeze, your palms turned up
        in prayer, a dove on your arm, a lamb at your feet.
        Francis,

I saw you once for sale at Gardener's Supply
        preaching to hose-reels, marigolds, ornamental
        deer.

With devotion,

Dear Francis, Rebuilder of San Damiano,

If the Word became flesh, why not
        that crucifix become voice?
Some will wonder how, but in the end
        I believe. After all,

what else turns a rich, Crusade-bound
        knight into a beggar
of bread and stones who kissed lepers'
        sores for the glory

of God? I wonder what the Umbrian
        would have thought
who painted the loin-clothed Christ
        on that Syrian-style

cross San Damiano's penniless priest
        lacked funds to repair,
or what that priest thought when,
        leaving, you curled

a costly sum into his hands, had
        him promise not to let
the altar candle die, then took off
        like a wild man—stunned,

obsessed, undone. High on the voice
of the Lord, you danced
through the fields toward town, madly
concocting one hell of a plan.

From one who also hears voices

Dear Son of Pietro Bernardone,

Nicodemus had nothing on you:

When he heard, *You must be born again,*
        he wondered how on earth
to climb back inside his mother's womb,

but you knew precisely what to do: remove
        your clothes in the public
square, by your nakedness loudly, irrevocably

declare whose you were, whose you chose
        to be. It was a start, and though
the bishop tried to spare you shame, protect

your rich father's name with his holy golden
        robe, hide your tender
olive frame, you refused. Instead, walked

shoeless toward the winter woods wearing
        nothing but a hair-shirt
and a song (in French, no less). Priest

to beggars and sparrows, hills, and the lilies
        of the fields, it wasn't long
before the lepers took you for their own.

Francis, what was it like to finally belong?

With admiration,

Dear Francesco,

I too take long walks in the fields and woods.
        Sometimes, I must confess,
I even speak secretly to birds. I'm not at all sure

        what they think, though I love
the way the robin cocks its head. The squirrels
        pay no heed, and moles keep

poking passages through leaves. By the brook
        is a bank where, every time
I pass, a snake cuts through the yellow grass

        and stops me short, then waits,
stone still, while I move on. There sways a pine
        so tall and full of sky it seems

to know my name. Francesco, sometimes I want
        to make the woods my home, give
myself wholly to the kingdom of balsam and stars,

        but I am inclined to a table and bed,
four walls and a stove, pipes, a sink, and a roof
        of rusting tin. Brother minor,

I too have heard the call of the thrush—
     the difference between you
and me is this: at the end of my walk I come in.

Sincerely,
An insider

Dear Barefoot Friend,

I am pressing my toes in soil
and morning grass wet with shade,

collecting beans barefoot among
the weeds. Against skin, the patio

is all pebble and grit, the floor-
boards in the potting shed damp.

I do not approach the garbage bin
for fear of broken glass. Francis,

I find it hard to believe giving
up shoes was no passing fad, not

a summertime thing. Exactly what
was the point? To be like the poor

or feel the tender grip of the earth?
Perhaps, like a pilgrim, you wished

to draw closer to Christ. Shoeless,
you blessed the cobbles of Gubbio

and Greccio with your naked heels,
hallowed the smooth marble floors

of St. Peter's in Rome—the dusty,
sun-hammered roads of Syria

and Spain. It seems everywhere
you walked was holy ground. But

didn't snow and ice chill and cut?
Did stones and roots not make

you bleed? Tell me, when Sister
Death arrived to sweep you home,

did she tisk you for playing rough
with the sacred temple of God, or

praise you for bearing your cross?
Forgive me, Francis: I can't help

but think your days were too brief,
that two leather soles bound with

laces or straps might have added
a couple more years to your life.

Shoe-clad

Dear Francis,

I have fractured my navicular
    watering plants. From the counter

to the table, the table
    to the bathroom—all travel

has become a pilgrimage
    of sorts. You must have cut

your fingers hauling stones
    through Assisi's cobbled streets,

then down the hill. Did you twist
    your wrists from the weight

of the bricks? I imagine you crushed
    a few toes, but—as penance

for your knighthood dreams
    (not to mention the cloth

you stole)—positively refused
    to let anyone know. If good

has come of my injured foot
    (and—I hesitate to add—sprained

left thumb), it is this: the catbird
    has become my friend. I have learned

to love his sometimes frog-like call
   (though he has yet to actually appear).

And now I have more time to write
   these lines to you, Francis. I fear

for those who have no time to think,
   no cause to pray. What do you say

to one who has never been broken?
   To unfired, un-shattered clay?

With hope,
Injured

Dear Lord of the Revels,

The clink's not always what it seems. Paul
remade his cell a church, a place of praise—
whittled psalms and sent them ringing off

the rough-hewn walls, the iron chains. They
say you were good for a joke even here—
here on stone as cold as doubt, here on hay

rank with grief. Perhaps a single shaft of light
at noon. Perhaps a single crust of moldy rye.
The shiver started somewhere in your feet,

then gripped your knees and spine, settled
in your lungs. Now the cough that drummed
against the damp was yours, not his—soldier

in the corner cursing Christ, nor his—geyser
with a beard of drool and blood. No wool
for warmth, no fire, you turned to words,

doled them out like a drunk at a feast, like
a lush who lifts his mug to every guest
and then the dog and then the king and then

the moon. Lord of the Revels, you took on
the dark, dueled fear with the artful sword
of your tongue, made light of war, of want,

the perpetual stink of unwashed men. Who
knows precisely what you said, what turn
of phrase wrung laughter out of gloom (or

did you sing?). Who knows precisely when
a grin appeared across the cell, an upturned
lip, a sparkling eye. No lightning struck,

no walls came down, no angel showed
to blind the guard or break the lock or slip
a key, but there in the airless, echoing dark

a muffled snort, a slap on the thigh. Jester-
turned-saint: you baptized with gags, jokes,
puns—and taught yourself how to be free.

Captivated

Dear Lover of Lady Poverty,

When you broke with the world, you gave up jerkins and boots
        (Italian leather, no less),

the title to your name. In light of your example, I hereby forsake
        (not wanting to duplicate)

the paisley, polarized shades I have wanted to buy for some months
        (now on sale at Rite Aid),

plans for a new voile spread and matching shams—you see, my room
        (unaltered in years)

is begging for a complete re-do. In addition, I forthwith happily resign
        (and with only a little shame)

my ignorance of bird songs, apathy toward insects, and above all else
        (no simple task)

my solemn right to complain—about weather, fractures, vacuuming
        (the Lord gives),

or the sudden need for new axles, a change of plans, someone to love
        (the Lord takes away).

I'd also like to swear off phones, hornets, gas stations, wars,
        (and while I'm at it)

the banality of prose. When it comes to relinquishing clothes, I can
        (most definitely)

do without nylons and heels and that black bridesmaid shawl I prized
        (but never wore),

hung up in my closet for years. Abandoning these worldly goods
        (I sincerely trust)

will help me be a little more like you. If I could, I'd even give up politicians
        (and bad news).

In truth, Francis, there are many things I'd like to lose.

Encumbered by stuff

Dear Francesco of Assisi,

The nuns serve us leek and garlic soup in white
bowls with silver spoons round as the moon
and deep. I sketch the poplars from the window,
rows of lavender, listen to the hills. We walk

the cobbles, gaze up at tall shutters painted sand
and rose through which, the guidebook tells us,
you launched your father's silks and fine French
cloths. The air in the church is damp—cave-like

and old. Ochre is the cross that hangs beneath
a yellow light, brown the hooded frocks of friars
who sandal past and speak low tones. Five or six
squeeze in a car—dented, blue, and rimmed

with rust. We stare and stare, try not to laugh—
now we know that monks can drive! But what
is really on my mind is this: gelati. Never before
have I seen such pinks and mauves and limes:

lemon, coffee, almond, melon, fig—each striking
its own private deal with the eye. On the fifth day
or so we finally give in—point at the glass and treat
our tongues to a taste of the town you called home.

Then on to the basilica to see your tomb. I am ten,
and the air is calling my name. When we board
the bus to take us down the hill to the train, I believe
in knights and voices, miracles and saints.

With fond memories,

Dear Wolf-whisperer,

That you proposed a pact with a wolf
    should make me think you

mad. So devoted to the cause of peace,
    it struck you blind. Why not spill

your blood halting the Crusades and win
    a martyr's crown? (Some say you left

for Egypt with just that in mind.) Instead
    you wagered all on a howling dog

and the sign of the cross. Gubbio was up
    in arms, the points of whittled sticks

and pikes flashing in the streets. But leave
    it to you, my friend, you and your

lofty, chivalrous truce. First you rebuked
    the beast, then tendered a pledge.

It should have slayed you on the spot
    in that sun-dappled wood. It should

have shredded your lark-brown frock, but,
    charmed by your voice (did you sing

to it by chance?), it agreed to live on gifts
      of meat and cause no undue harm.

Some say it raised its paw to seal the deal.
      I'd call this a tale, the kind men spin

when they want the pope to make a man
      a saint, but how to explain wolf bones

unearthed in Gubbio chapel's crypt?

A coming-around cynic

Dear Francis,

There is something to be said for B-grade films
about the lives of saints—the kinds with dubbed
voices and stiff scripts and shafts of light descending
from the clouds into warm pools of holiness in which
only a chosen few will ever be bathed. The black
eye-liner is thick, and you can almost see the giant
droning fans whipping up miracles from just off screen,
and the fog machine going about its hallowed
work. Actors with lake-blue eyes and flaxen, unkempt
hair gaze skyward as they walk. So light their step,
so even their pace (like angels), they seem to carry

no actual weight. They greet danger with a calm so
baroque it might be taken for joy, and they do not sigh
or flinch at pain—whether stubbing a toe on a wayward
root or burning at the stake. The soundtrack loops
and you forget there were no violins in 900 A.D.
(though if a saint can hear the voice of God, why not
hear an orchestra as well?). Francis, did you know
you speak English and have red hair on TV? Ettore
Bassi plays you with flair, though on YouTube his words
and lips are gravely out of sync. But what is faith,
after all, if not the willing suspension of disbelief?
Which is why I loved these overdone commercial-
sprinkled films that made me cry as I child as I
watched the credits roll on Sunday nights, late, when
the house had fallen still, and my parents had long
been asleep. God bless the hair-dressers, sound-mixers,
colorists, grips—the gaffers who wired the sets, the men

who raised the cranes. God bless the blue-eyed actors
who taught me how to believe: their profiles glowing
in backlit prayer, tunics rippling in the artificial breeze.

Starry-eyed

Dear Francis,

When it comes to living small,
you were ahead of your time,
which is why I nominate you
patron saint of tiny homes.
Think chapel for one on wheels
with cedar floors, a loft to sleep,
and a skylight in the roof. Here
is where I'd go to pray and where
I pray to live (pending a friend
to let me squat and the zoning
board's OK). In short, Francis,
it's a new way of being poor.
I hope you will approve.

A simplicity-seeker

Dear Holy Traveler
(on the occasion of your first visit to the Vatican),

Did wanderlust
       send you to Rome,
or your mother, Pica,
who must have thought it would do you
            some good?

How many heads
       turned at the sound
of the coins

you dropped on Saint Peter's tomb?
          Did you fling

that silver
       through the iron grate
for the thrill
of its tinny ring through chancel,
          transept, tower,

chapel, nave—
       the vast, echoing heart
of Constantine's own
bold, marble-columned declaration
          of faith?

Do you think
       the apostle approved
of such a temple

for his grave—gold mosaics, statues,
                a confessio—

and, above all else,
         that fixed ritual
of blessing
his bones with the strewing of coins?
             How strange

that soon on a hill
        in the town
you were born,
a basilica grand as Rome would rise
          in *your* name.

A sightseer

Dear Reluctant Saint,

I imagine your heavenly tasks must keep you rather occupied, but if you find the need to get away, Assisi might be nice for a short stay. Here's what you do: from the *Porta Nuova* car park, ride the escalator to the city gate. This will save you no small amount of sweat. From the *Piazza Santa Chiara,* be sure to take in the sweeping views—in particular the valley's famous olive groves (a great spot for a selfie or two). When your pilgrim feet find they need a rest, the steps of the *Santa Maria* and a *bacio* gelato should suffice. Be warned: as you near the basilica, souvenir stands will increase. Prepare to feel somewhat mocked and displaced by bobbleheads, dog tags, shaving mugs, mouse pads—all sporting the image of your twelfth-century face. And then there are glow-in-the-dark rosary beads—cheap relics for those "flash-in-the-pan Francis fans," in the words of Rick Steves. When you reach the top of the "Hill of Hell"—where, in your day, the worst of criminals met their fate—you will have arrived at the most frequented shrine of any canonized saint. Download a brochure for a self-guided tour, and don't miss Giotto's frescos— "stunning" per the *New York Times* (though they may in fact be the work of another man's hand, *Fodor's* explains). Of course, no visit is complete without checking out the crypt. And one more thing: don't forget to bring some euros along. Everything costs a fee except, of course, the view. Plus, you will want spare change to tip the washroom attendant who hands out paper and keeps the seats clean—not to mention a few good-luck coins to throw on your tomb.

Your willing tour guide

Dear Lover of Light,

There lived a priest
so in love with light
it drove him mad.
Paint was his thing.
When he could no longer
preach, he hopped a train
south, took up a brush,
turned zinc and lead
and chrome
into gaudy, wild-
petaled ambassadors
of the dawn. He slapped
stars as big as brooches
on the sky, danced
crows across bowing fields
of wheat, exalted a bowl
of onions, a bridge, a pipe,
a chair, a bed. Postmen
and prostitutes
were his friends—
so too were irises,
almond trees,
windmills,
clouds. Francis,
if you think of a painting
as a kind of song, he too
canticled the sun.

A Vincent enthusiast

Dear Francesco, Confidante,

I never understood the notion of make-believe,
especially when it comes to a friend. What good
is someone who is not actually there? I'd rather
talk to the birds. Give me a beetle, a damselfly,
or better yet, an oak. A hammock makes for a faithful
chum, not to mention the refrain of a favorite song.
And I am not above calling the sun my brother. If
I had my druthers, I might even chat with the saints;
they companion me when I read about them in books—
I love their holy words. Francis, I cannot say for sure
these letters will reach their intended destination,
but how grateful I am that you are beyond a doubt
for real—not my lonely mind's madcap invention.

A kindred spirit

Dear Dreamer,

"If we had possessions, we would need weapons
and laws to defend them,"

you told the bishop, who must have thought you
mad to give up armor,

clothing, horses, furniture, clocks. But you had
a point. Me, I'm not so rich

as to need fancy locks, alarms, or—God forbid—
a gun to protect my goods.

Most all I have is passed down or a thrift-store
find. If there's anything

I have a lot of, it's books, and who wants those?
But here's the thing:

the stove needs scrubbing, and the oven sometimes
too. Whenever I look,

the counters and sinks are crying out for bleach.
Laundry mounts, mirrors

streak: I need an arsenal of weapons to defend
against dust, oil stains, odors,

grime. Detergent, for one—a vacuum, a dustpan,
a broom, sponges and rags,

a soap to remove spots, a spray to clean glass,
a special cloth to polish

jewelry and another to polish shoes. Francis, it's
a maddening game I play

and almost always lose. You, on the other hand,
had the sky for a house—trees,

a field, a cave. You owned the wind and the sun:
your prize possessions

were a song and a dream. These you never had
to defend, never had to clean.

A neat freak

Dear Francis (with all due respect),

There is a difference
between a man
                and a saint:

one gets a plum-
colored bruise
                when he falls.

The next day
it turns sea-green.
                He finds out

the twist was more
than a sprain,
                but a fracture

requiring
a certain type of cast.
                He prays

insurance
will cover the cost.
                The other

has orchids
for eyes, false blue
                as a Hallmark

sky. He glows, lit
from within—a light bulb
                        must be on

under his skin.
Everything he looks at
                        turns to spring,

though he himself
can never age, can never sing
                        or break

a bone. Stuck in plastic,
gazing up
                        in praise—

perfect, peaceful, mute:
in a wallet sleeve he spends
                        his days.

A mortal

Dear Francesco, the Lord's Mendicant,

To be frank, I never understood
your choice to beg (why not
at least *grow* your food?) until
I broke my foot and the fridge
went low—nothing left but a few
limp greens and a covered dish
of hard-boiled eggs. I knew
what I had to do: call across the street
with my bold request, apologies,
and a rather lengthy list. At four,
there was a knock at the door,
and before I could stand, Angela
came in, loaded up the fridge
with meat and milk, zucchini,
black olives, and cheese—said
she once put out her knee, had had
to stay in bed. Unlike you, I paid—
wrote her out a check—and yet,
seeing my table massed with goods
another had acquired—tomatoes,
butter, eggplant, almonds, beans—
I understood your wish to beg:
to pray and ask a man to share
his bread, then with thankfulness
to eat yields joy that can't be had
another way.

A beggar

Dear Francis, Peacemaker,

A thousand dead in the Gaza Strip.
How much weeping

                    can those hills hold?

I know what is a gun, a rocket,
a mine, but not

                    this: an instrument

of peace. If you would, Francis,
please elucidate.

                    A bullet bores a hole

through bone, but what tool,
iron or wood,

                    can heal a stone,

breathe life into an unseen
wound? The blood

                    of Egypt called

your name: you disembarked
shoeless, unarmed

                    but for a song

and a fool's truce: no silver,
no offer—

                    only your heart

rendered: a balm of oil to pour
on enemy heads—

                              on hair and beards

black as crow, black as schorl,
shiny and black

                              and holy

as your own. Tell me, friend,
would you

                              have done it again?

With concern,   43

Dear Francis
(on the occasion of Christmas),

About time
you put on
a show—
juggler,
troubadour,
lover of jokes.
Did you know
the whole town
would process
through
the streets,
up the hill past
the church, past
the fields,
to that cave
where, for actors,
you borrowed
an ox and an ass,
for props
a farmer's
spare hay?
A girl
with pure eyes
and flowing
black hair—
a goatherd,
perhaps—

you bid her
to stay
and stand
alongside
a gentle-
faced man
with strong,
weathered
hands
and a cloak
of gray wool.
An old
wooden trough
you set
in between,
moved the ox
to the left, placed
some lanterns
up front.
And then
you sang,
and the torch
flames danced,
and the hills
stood watch,
and the stars
came out.

Peace,

Dear Brother,

Since Clare eloped at night,
        it must have been by the light
            of candles
and torches she breathed
her vows,
        said for good

whose she was.

Glowing the cross, quiet
          the friars standing in the shadows
            to watch.
Or did they sing?

What color was the trust
        in her eyes when you whispered
           a prayer, then lifted
her hair and snipped
its flaxen waves,

offered her a veil of wool?

Outside, a veil of stars—
        a different kind of light.
           Did you know
it was the wedding night
of a saint
        when you knelt with her

on stone, then led her
        by the arm through sleeping fields
            and unlit woods,
past hillside caves,

through a hushed and constellated dark
        to the convent

where she would be safe?

From one who has never taken vows

Dear Lover of Solitude,

I cook for one,
eat to the sound of NPR droning on
and on. I find it hard

to take the time to read—
so much to do: and then there's the web,
that pixilated land

I go to to glean
the news of friends I haven't seen in years:
David changed his profile pic,

Lindsay splattered coffee
on the cat, it's Jillian's kid's first day of school.
I'm considering a new rule:

shut off this stream
of sound and light by eight—perhaps before—
and give myself wholly

to an unsuspecting book
until it has become my friend. Francis, I wish
to dwell in just one place

for long enough to catch
my breath, sift some little truth and hold it
to the light like a scintillating

gem—then maybe I'd find
enchantment in the hush, learn to love
this solo life again.

As ever,
Alone

Dear Francis,

There's a wonder you may not have heard tell of
or seen. It stops time: hours can pass in a clock's
single tick. It turns night into day. It even (sort of)
thinks. Any task I wish help with, I simply ask:
how to spell a word, check my oil, remove a stain,
find a date. Given a certain number, it delivers
in a day precisely what I need: socks, ballet tickets,
headphones, the *Sunday Times,* jeans. It's pretty swell
with information too: it knows the languages of
fish, the distance of the sun, the shelf-lives of chèvre
and brie. *Sounds implausible,* I can almost hear
you say, but by this wonder's power, I can actually
inhabit two places at once. From my room, I have
tracked monarchs in Belize, pedaled the Golden
Gate Bridge, people-watched at Parisian cafés.
In fact, Francis, I just swung by your tomb, where
the faithful are finishing mass. Did I mention this
wonder anesthetizes pain? It has rendered me numb
for hours on end, and when levity's the medicine
I need, it's always good for a laugh or two. Here's
the clincher: I'm devoted—and I don't even like
the damn thing. It steals my praise with hardly
my knowing, holds me in its grip like a hungry
white-tailed hawk. Francis, I dare you to offer it
an hour—or three. When you try to escape its grasp—
may you meet with more than beginner's luck.

A reluctant idol-worshipper

Dear Friend of the Wild,

      "Decoupled from nature"—
That's what the *New York Times*
               calls it, this state of life
               detached from things
that leaf and buzz,
      bloom
               and fly.
      It's divorce outright.
We forget we are wedded to the earth,
               wonder why we feel
               disowned. Francis,
would you believe
      some children
               hardly ever
      leave their homes—have yet
to see a snake part grass, touch
               the warm nose
               of a horse, pass
a few hours in a tree. Nature Deficit
      Disorder—
               NDD:
      That's the technical term
for trading woods and sky for screens,
               sun for LEDs,
               forgetting
how to wander fields, turn over
      logs,

                                collect
                   caterpillars or maple keys.
           What a waste of toads and creeks
                              and Queen Anne's
                            lace, of worms
           and rain and mud. It seems to me
                      a kind
                                   of sin,
                    this slap in the face
           to all that's wild and green, this chronic
                              staying in.

An advocate for wonder

Dear Francis,

A man
lived in a cabin
he built in the woods
by a particular
pond,
planted an acre
of beans
and wrote
what it was like
to turn his back
on the world—
at least for a time—
to live life deep.
He collected
sounds—
owls, rails,
whippoorwills,
bells—and
two full years
of pine-soaked
thought.
I admit
I have always
admired
his pluck.
Would that

you two
could have
taken
a walk.

A Walden fan

Dear Patient Saint,

With my foot in a cast, so much
                    remains on hold:

fall sweaters piled on the trunk
to be sold to the Essex Clothes Exchange

will simply have to wait, as will
                  the showerhead,

which I managed to break with the weight
of a pair of dripping wet jeans. Then

there is the closet I have been wanting
               to excavate. Thanks

to the neighbors (who delivered milk
and greens, took out my trash, and even

helped me pick my crop of yellow beans),
              I am well supplied.

Strange, but I simply have no needs. It seems
life will go on fine whether or not I actually

clean. If the shower is not fixed, so what?
              I've come to love

the new way I bathe. Now all I've put on hold
for years—to read and write and simply sit

beneath the oak for hours, watch the wind
                    extrapolate the leaves—

has come to count for everything. In sum,
I no longer fear not getting things done.

Contented

Dear Francis,

I have never prayed in a cave,
but once I ran down a highway before dawn
to encounter God in a particular field.

A trooper stopped to ask if I was OK,
said someone had called. My sundress
must have tipped them off—not running gear

for sure—but I had had no time to think
when the moon was still out and I suddenly woke
compelled to up and go. Where? I did not know

until, walking down the road in the ash-gray
light, I recalled a date I had failed to keep
with the sun on a particular hill—but now,

in order to watch it rise, I'd have to run, fly
those two or three miles, my sundress flapping
like a tunic or frock. How would I know

if I had met with God? I could not say.
The field was mist and the sky stone gray—
it was a clouded start, a break of day with no

clear break save a porthole in the clouds,
a fist of luminous peach, and I stood in my dress
in the cool of the mist and saw with my eyes

the gleam of that orb. Its honey-thick shine,
as it poked through the hole, seemed to stop
for a time, and then slipped by. What chance

that vent would meet the sun, the sun cross by
the small round breach? Was I the only one
to watch this miracle of sorts? I'd come to greet

the sun, but instead it greeted me. Francis,
was the miracle the way the sun cut past
that perfect cleft, or that I was there to see?

58 | *Your fellow pilgrim*

Dear Francis
(on the occasion of your surgery),

A blazing rod is no instrument of peace.
        If violence could heal, your consent

I might grasp, but it seems to me you lacked
        the will to decline what others

deemed best. You bowed to the doctor's word
        like a child—offered yourself,

were willing to lose. Was it for glory—the kind
        that comes from a burning zeal

to obey—or for your brothers' sakes, who failed
        to see your blindness as a gift, whose

only way to love was through constraint? The dark
        had taught you how to sing, transformed

the sun from source of light to friend. The art
        of thanks was yours to craft, yours

the time to listen to the leaves. You hardly believed
        in that so-called cure, so why let them

brand your temple veins? Did you see it as a test?
        You knew the chill of worn-out lungs,

the probing pain of nails. Each day you dressed
    your bleeding hands and feet, held

your bandaged side. You were unafraid of scars.
    Stars were what you lived for now—

the wind, cicadas, sister moon, who soothed
    your wounds with luminous songs

no one else could hear. *Brother, be kind,* you said
    to the fire as they drew from the coals

the flame-red tongs.

From one who has also been burned

Dear Francis,

I would like to meet Job. By chance,
have you bumped into him up there?

What did he say about misery and loss,
the state of his health? Did he comment

on his tactless friends, what it was like
rubbing ashes in his wounds? The stench

of his sores and the curse of his wife—
it must have been more than his pious

heart could bear. Pray tell me his trick,
how he managed to pull through, keep

faith on a hair-thin thread of hope. When
sleep was a lie, relief a dream, what well

did he draw his patience from? Francis,
if in that vast expanse you come across

this luckless man, convey my very best
regards and kindly tell him this: though

we have not met or talked, I feel I can
relate to him. I consider Job a friend.

In need of hope

Dear Francis
(on the occasion of your stigmata),

As if
you could
know
why a seraph
should appear,
why its six
dazzling wings
should enfold
the dying Christ.
As if
you could ask
the mountain's
jutting rocks
what provoked
those lonely hills
to illuminate
your fast.
Because
I cannot say
why love and pain
go hand in hand,
I will not
doubt
the sky
tore up
in flames,
that day of joy

and blood—
nor that
you bore
His wounds.

From one unpierced

Dear Wounded Saint,

After the nails, the hush
       of a seraph's wings as you lay
       on the grass in the hold of those luminous

arms—your eyes three-quarters
       closed, your head turned slightly
       back. In the distance, a smooth and lonely moon-

glossed pond. Caravaggio
       made a study of your hands,
          fingers curled in an open clutch around your

unseen wounds: the right
       just below a tear in your frock
       where the sword-tip pierced your side, the left

cupping a prayer, palm up—
       even as it dangles down in pain.
       Some say the love of God can cause a man

to faint, plow him down,
       drive him mad, take him
       wholly to the ground. That force that filled

the void with breath unhinged
       a Hebrew's hip, struck a Roman blind,
       but you had nothing left to lose that night the sky

called out your name—nothing
to lose but yourself to the wild of a love
the stars had never seen, the blazing hills could not

explain. Life held no claim
on you now, the artist knew, so
he rendered you half-dead, laid out as Christ

in Mary's arms, only here
a seraph holds your wilted frame,
supports your tilted head above his angled knee.

His wings are close, | 65
the feathers soft and real.
They ruffle in the cool of the late-night breeze.

A student of Renaissance art

Dear Friend,

Look—I can walk! This is no small thing.
The lame man whom Jesus healed—I feel

I can relate to him. See how light my step
even though I have to limp (and crutches

are still requisite). My foot, that useless,
dangling thing that turned me off a stair

and flung me on concrete—at long last—
now bears my weight. My ally once again,

my trusted, kindred friend. No longer
will I spend my days alone, apart, on leave.

Believe it or not, I can drive. No more
asking for rides, sending friends to town

for food. Amazing: anything I need
or want I'll simply go and buy. Perhaps

tomorrow I'll swing by the lake, catch
some sun and the mountain view. Next,

I'll return a few overdue books, pick up
some *forever* stamps. There's clothing

to sell, a showerhead to fix, closets to clean.
My life is back again and I'm spilling thanks,

but with it comes a fear I can't explain—
Francis, what if all I've learned has been in vain?

Worried

Dear Francis,

A fine playwright once asked, *Does anyone
realize life while they live it?*

    No, he answered. *Saints and poets
maybe. They do some.* And men of the stage,

I would add—those daring, lime-lit souls
who script kisses and brawls,

    miracles and loss until the world
stops spinning for a moment and finally makes

sense. Take, for instance, the bard, who sewed
lines into scenes, scenes into lives—dressed up

    men in boots and velvet vests—or rags—
sent them onto a torch-illumined set in a glorified,

globe-shaped barn. If we are all the stuff of dreams,
then dreams are real, which—it seems to me—

    you proved extravagantly well, rehearsing
your tragic-comic farce: grittier and nobler

and more dazzling than the rest. You were not
afraid to put on a show, don burlap and a rope,

cut your hair, lose your leather shoes, wax
eloquent about the white-fire stars, the sighing wind—

even sing. You and your brown-clad chums took on
the roles of drunks and fools—the proverbial comic

relief. Only this: if you were drunk, Francis,
it was on the riotous love of God. Your audience

was the sky, a few lepers, a crow. You wrote
the script as you went along—soliloquies galore—

and when the curtain dropped, the stage
went dark, you took your bow and slept, and the world

went on, blind and dull and less one thespian-saint
who dared to play his part.

A theater buff

Dear Jongleur de Dieu,

When your lungs failed
      and your sight was all but gone, you took on
      a new kind of work: you canticled
           the sun.

What was there to do
      but dress and redress your unhealed wounds,
      wait in a cave for the hours to pass,
           the threat

of daylight to fade?
      And so you sang—lute-less, illumined by praise
      and the psalms of mountain birds.
           When you heard

the news—the bishop's rift
      with a lifelong friend—you penned an extra verse,
      sent a friar to town on a mission
           to sing.

Who would have guessed
      the offender to kneel, the bishop forgive at the sound
      of a hymn—no less, a ballad to the sun?
           The pope

had reasons for making you
>   a saint. With respect, I have my own: you sewed
>   a handful of words to a tune and changed
>   the world with a song.

An idealist

Dear Francis
(on the occasion of your death),

How long
it takes
a man
to walk
a mile,
I cannot say.
An ash-
gray cloth
Jacoba
wrapped
you in,
but first,
the brothers
laid you
on the ground,
naked
as the day
you learned
to breathe,
naked
as the silver
coins
you owed,
naked
as the thief
upon the cross.
As you

closed
your
darkened
eyes,
I like
to think
you heard
the
insects'
evening
songs,
a minuet
of rustling
leaves,
the lisping
wings
of gathering
larks.

Godspeed

Epilogue

When Sister Death approached, Francis asked to be laid on the ground naked—his final embrace of poverty. His skin communing with the Umbrian earth, Francis breathed his last as the brothers sang hymns and watched on. Witnesses record that during these moments just after sunset on October 3, 1226, larks gathered in the skies. Francis held a special affinity for these plain, earth-toned birds who, to him, symbolized humility and simplicity. In his biography of Francis, G. K. Chesterton writes, "It has been said that animals are sometimes conscious of things to which man . . . is for the moment blind." How fitting that the man who honored animals more than any other figure in recorded Christian history was, at his death, honored by them.

A Roman noblewoman named Jacoba, who had donated property to Francis for use as a leper hospice and whom he endearingly referred to as "Brother Jacoba," supplied a shroud in which to wrap the saint's body. The brothers buried him in the Church of San Giorgia, one of three churches, including San Damiano, that Francis and his followers had painstakingly restored. Two years later, construction started in Assisi on a papal basilica in honor of Francis, and his remains were transported to the basilica in 1230, the year Pope Gregory IX canonized Francis a saint.

When Francis died, many were already following his radical example, having given up wealth and possessions to serve lepers and devote themselves to lives of faith. Over time, the number of

Francis-followers grew steadily, and today, Franciscans comprise the largest religious order in the Catholic Church, with communities around the globe—among them the Poor Clares, who follow the example of Clare in embracing Francis's rule of poverty. But Francis's reach stretches beyond formal religious communities and the walls of the Catholic Church. Ordinary people of all backgrounds embrace his example of simplicity, his reverence for nature, his dedication to serving the poor, his commitment to peacemaking, and his desire to be a fool for God. Few have left as lasting a mark as the crusader and cloth merchant's son from Assisi who heard a different call.

A Conversation with the Author

How did you come to write this book, and why did you choose to address your letters to Saint Francis?

I have long been intrigued by the strange and wonderful life of Saint Francis. The fascination started when I was ten years old. My family spent a week in Assisi while we were living in Europe during my father's sabbatical. We stayed in a convent and explored the hilltop village on foot, and I suddenly realized that Saint Francis was not a garden statue but an actual historical figure. Though we were only tourists, it felt like we were pilgrims as we visited the San Damiano cross, where Francis heard God call him to rebuild the church, and the basilica, where Giotto's famous thirteenth-century frescoes tell the story of the saint's life—and where Francis is buried. Learning about the life of Francis by walking the cobbled streets he walked, visiting the dimly lit churches he prayed in, and viewing 700-year-old frescoes painted high up on cathedral walls was unforgettably magical.

Fast forward to a few years ago when I read a captivating series of letters to William Blake authored by the contemporary Canadian poet Susan McCaslin. I immediately knew I wanted to write a series of letters to someone in history as well, and the first person who came to mind was Saint Francis. But my knowledge of Francis was limited to what I had learned roaming the streets of Assisi as a ten-year-old. So I checked some biographies out of the library, including G. K. Chesterton's, which became a favorite, and for fun, I looked up a few movies about Saint Francis to watch as well. A few days after starting my research—perhaps fortuitously—I broke my foot while watering plants. Immobilized, I unexpectedly found myself with a great deal of time on my hands—time to read, think, write, and dream. There is nothing like an injury to slow you down and give you a chance to take inventory of your life. And, for a writer, there is nothing like being stuck in one place alone for long periods of time with good books to spark your imagination. And so *A Gathering of Larks* was born.

What intrigues you most about Francis of Assisi?

I think the majority of people who find themselves drawn to him admire his special way with animals and, more generally, his deeply spiritual connection with nature. These aspects of Francis appeal to me as well, but what appeals most is his free-spirited shirking of all that hindered him from living the gospel as he understood it. Francis was in love with God and God's world, and he was willing to be a fool for that love. If people followed him, it wasn't because he wanted to start a movement but because he wanted to live a boldly authentic life of faith—loving people across social barriers and valuing simplicity and poverty over prestige and wealth. To some, Francis must have appeared as ungrateful and absurd, walking away from his inheritance to wander the fields and live with the poor, but to others, he furnished a compelling example of what it looks like to follow that carpenter from Nazareth who had no pillow on which to rest his head.

Is there anything else that particularly intrigues you about Francis?

As a writer, I am also intrigued that Francis valued crafting poems and songs as part of his vocation. He did not leave behind his troubadour ways when he decided to live for God, but he became a troubadour for God. A hopeless romantic, Francis was not afraid to follow his heart, and he devoted significant time to joyfully converting what was in his heart into art. I love that when Francis made his break with his family's wealth—and his clothes—in the public square, he didn't walk away in silence—he walked away singing. Witnesses tell us that when he addressed crowds or gave a sermon, he frequently broke into song. Nearly eight hundred years later, we are still singing his words.

What are your thoughts on the value of letters—historically and today?

Letters are intimate, reflective, and deeply personal communications, offering a privileged window into a person's thoughts, feelings, and life. They balance spontaneity and introspection in a way that emails, texts, and social media posts do not. Electronic communication, by definition, lacks privacy—with a click, it can be forwarded, shared, or printed. And its content is mediated by an impersonal, standardized typeface made up of pixels on an illuminated screen. Letters, on the other hand, inhabit space: you hold them in your hands, touching the same paper the letter-writer handled. Transit time, while regarded as an inconvenience by some, adds value in my opinion. Another added value is the letter-writer's unique handwriting. Whether flowery and elegant or quirky and crude, ink scrawled on a folded piece of paper is a token of the letter-writer's personality and presence, and that token is ultimately a gift.

Comparatively, electronic communications are cheap, and, not surprisingly, we write them much differently than we write letters. Emails and texts do not carry our spirit in the same way. We simply do not entrust our hearts to computers, iPads, and smartphone screens to the extent that people once entrusted their hearts to their pens and stationery. The death of letter-writing is a great loss.

Do you see letters ever coming back?
Will people write letters again as they once did?

I don't think letter-writing will ever return to its historical status. Every now and then I meet someone who intentionally carves out time to write letters, even if only on a few occasions a year. For these people, writing letters is akin to a spiritual practice, and I admire that. Few, however, seem to have the time or interest. Images have become the primary cultural currency of our day, largely displacing words. To digital natives, letters are wholly foreign and obsolete. But I do see a romance of the letter slowly percolating in literature. In the past decade, a number of books have showcased fictional correspondences, and recently, a memoir written in the form of letters has been published to critical acclaim.

I'm intrigued by letters as a literary form because I believe they have something unique to offer—a freshness and an immediacy that can be hard to achieve in a story or novel. In some ways, they are a lot like poems because their value lies as much in the spaces they create as in the content they put forward. Letters don't tell a story, but together they can scaffold a story, which is what I have attempted to do here with *A Gathering of Larks*. I've created the framework, and the reader gets to do the filling in.

How did you go about writing A Gathering of Larks?

The first letter that appears in this book is in fact the first letter I wrote to Francis. My showerhead had broken and, as I describe in the letter, I was ladling water over my head from the bathtub faucet to wash. At first this felt primitive and awkward, but then it felt luxurious and even strangely spiritual. There was something waterfall-like and baptismal about pouring liberal amounts of water over my shoulders and head. What is more, I began to picture people in times past and in other parts of the world washing this way, using only a bucket and a cup, and I felt a kind of kinship with them. But how do you communicate an experience like this to someone you know? To a friend's ears, it would sound either childish and silly or laughably sentimental. So I began to craft a letter in my head, experimenting with the idea of describing this somewhat mystical bathing experience to St. Francis.

At first, I hesitated to write this letter because bathing seemed like a rather ordinary and unsophisticated subject to write to a saint about—not to mention perhaps unfittingly sensual. But then I realized that Francis was all about the ordinary, the unsophisticated, and even the sensual. He who went barefoot, choosing to feel the earth under his skin; he who bathed in streams; and he who was not afraid to leave his clothes behind in the public square when he renounced his wealth—*he* would certainly understand the poetry of this broken showerhead experience. And so I went ahead and wrote this first letter to St. Francis, and over the course of the summer the rest followed.

What did you enjoy most about the process of writing this book?

Asking Francis questions is what I enjoyed most about writing these letters. I felt like I was stepping into his world as a friend and having a heart-to-heart conversation with him. I think the best conversations are the ones where we graciously ask—and are asked—good, thoughtful, and even hard questions. Such questions simultaneously challenge and nourish. They are not about mining for information but about investing in another person's flourishing. When we ask questions in this way, we give a person an opportunity to be known, and this is an act of love. A writer and friend who read an early draft of *A Gathering of Larks* told me that my letters to Francis are love letters. Indeed, perhaps they are. Perhaps this is why I ask Francis so many questions.

Why did you choose to write these letters
as poems rather than as prose?

Poetry is what comes most naturally to me. When I write prose, I feel compelled to revise and revise and revise until I have eliminated every unnecessary word, and what is left is a poem. I love the economy of words in a poem, their visual dance across a page, and their musicality—the possibilities they furnish for patterns of sound. I experimented with many different forms in *A Gathering of Larks.* For me, experimenting with form and sound is a kind of play. So is experimenting with line endings and length. A poet is always asking her poem what it can do without. You see, in a poem, no words are extraneous—every word matters. There is a unique honesty in poetry because of this. And so, in addition to being my natural preference, poetry seemed the most fitting genre when writing to a saint.

A theme that threads through your letters is brokenness: the broken showerhead, your broken foot, the brokenness of our world. What did you learn about brokenness during the process of writing these letters?

Brokenness is painful, humbling, and hard, but it furnishes an occasion for us to experience love and makes redemption possible. The summer I fractured my foot, I came face to face with my own weakness. That summer held disappointment and loneliness, but so much good came out of this experience for me—the least of which is this book. Stuck at home reading, writing, and observing the nature in my backyard from the fold-up chaise lounge my neighbor gave me, I found a richness I would not have experienced had I managed to avoid tripping on that bottom stair while watering my plants.

If we let it, I believe brokenness makes us more open to God, giving us new eyes to see him at work in our lives and in the world. It weans us from what is unimportant and teaches us to focus on what really matters. And we may learn that what really matters is not what we thought. Perhaps what really matters is listening to the catbird, learning to humbly receive the kindness of neighbors, reading and thinking and writing, and simply resting in God's grace. Or perhaps what really matters—as Saint Francis found—is loving lepers, rebuilding an abandoned church, and preaching to birds. Some of the most compassionate, life-giving people I know are the ones who have experienced the most brokenness. They are people who have let God use their brokenness to bring healing to the broken places in other people. I aspire to be like them.

These letters express a great deal of faith, but at times, they also express uncertainty and doubt. Do you see faith and doubt as polar opposites or as compatible, perhaps even necessary bedfellows?

I love that when Francis heard God's voice tell him to rebuild his church, he rashly sold his father's expensive fabrics to raise money for the rebuilding even though those fabrics were not his to sell. In his zeal to do good and obey God, he made a mistake, and he had to face that mistake. But great good came out of that. His public apology to his father and the return of his father's money in the town square became a stage for one of the most inspiring and storied conversions in history. It seems to me that faith without doubt is not faith at all, and I think Francis models a faith that leaves room for doubt. Francis did not have it fully together. He did a lot of deep soul-searching, working out his faith over the course of years of failures as well as successes, questions as well as answers.

A helpful metaphor for faith, I think, is conversation, which is what these letters are. They are a conversation with Francis, but ultimately, they are a conversation with my own heart. When I let myself converse truly and deeply with my heart—whether through reading, writing, walking and thinking, or prayer—I find that I am conversing with the creator of my heart, who invites me into conversation with him. In that conversation, I don't always come by the answers I set out to uncover, but I draw closer to the one who holds the answers, and that is enough.

Reader's Guide

In this book of letters, I ask Saint Francis questions about the events in his life, his choices, his mistakes, and ultimately, his faith. I wonder how Saint Francis's story speaks to your journey and what questions you might ask him about his life and times, or perhaps about your own. I trust this reader's guide offers a helpful jumping-off point for considering how the themes explored in the letters—nature, materialism, simplicity, beauty, brokenness, faith—resonate with you. And I trust it will spur thought about how Francis's life and faith might inform the way we live in the modern world today—a world that is starkly different from his and yet surprisingly the same.

Questions for Thought and Discussion

Have you ever had an experience where you discovered something profoundly spiritual in something especially ordinary? In the first letter, a broken showerhead leads to an unexpectedly rich experience: Having to ladle water from the faucet becomes a kind of baptism. Later, when the author breaks her foot, she learns to draw meaning and pleasure out of ordinary things, and her pain baptizes her, so to speak, into new experiences of contemplation and prayer. If you have broken a bone or suffered a temporary (or permanent) disability, what did you discover from the experience?

A turning point in the life of Saint Francis was when he notoriously kissed a leper. From others' perspectives, the act was ludicrous. Lepers were despised, considered not only cursed but also dangerous, as this deforming disease was highly contagious. Yet spontaneously showing care to a leper was the most concrete way Francis felt he could follow the gospel, and it helped him overcome his greatest fear. Have you ever felt compelled to do something good, but the people around you did not understand what you were doing or why you were doing it? How did it change you?

In the spirit of Saint Francis, the author determines to give up a number of worldly goods and attitudes, but she finds it impossible to give up everything she'd like to lose—phones, gas stations, wars. Think of a time when you lived without something—whether voluntarily or not—and found your life richer for it. What have you wished to do without but found impossible to give up?

Francis had a special affinity for animals—and they for him. He especially loved the humble lark, whose simple brown feathers are the color of earth, and who, according to witnesses of Francis's death, gathered in the skies on that early October evening when he breathed his last. Do you have a special affinity with a particular animal? What characteristics of this animal do you aspire to or admire? Would others see this animal as representative of you, or would they choose another—and if so, which?

When the author breaks her foot, she finds herself depending on neighbors and friends for help. They do her grocery shopping for her, take out her trash, and harvest her garden. When was the last time a neighbor or friend helped to meet a need of yours? Did you feel cared for? Was it difficult to ask for or receive this help? What did you learn about yourself or others through this experience?

In one of her letters, the author asks Francis to give her regards to Job. Her experience of suffering leads her to feel a kinship with the biblical character, and she tells Francis, "I consider Job a friend." Is there a biblical character, a saint, or a historical figure whom, though you have never met in person, you feel a special kinship with because of a shared experience? What about your life do you feel this person would understand?

Francis lived close to the earth, walking barefoot, often sleeping outside, and calling the sun "brother" and the moon "sister." Today, many of us suffer from what has been coined Nature Deficit Disorder. "We forget that we are wedded to the earth," the author remarks. What effect does spending time in nature have on you physically, emotionally, and spiritually? What is one special place in nature you go to from time to time—or would like to go to? What keeps you and those you love from spending time in the natural world?

At the age of ten, the author went to Assisi with her family, a visit that had a profoundly enchanting effect on her. By the end of the visit, she found herself believing in "knights and voices, miracles and saints." Similarly, as a slightly older youth, she found her budding faith fortified in an unexpected place: B-grade films about the lives of saints. Describe a childhood experience of enchantment that awakened in you a new or deeper capacity to believe.

In one letter the author tells Francis of the magical powers of screens, which can give us a thrilling sense of control and affirmation while, at the same time, holding us tightly in their addictive grip. After lamenting her own addiction, she signs off as "A reluctant idol-worshipper." Have you ever experienced screens as addictive? If so, what about screens and the Internet do you find so difficult to resist? What about them makes you also a reluctant worshipper?

Francis devoted a significant amount of his time and thought to writing songs—some of which we still sing today. One of his songs, when performed, led two prominent leaders in Assisi to reconcile their differences following an entrenched conflict. In your opinion, what is the value and power of art—whether song, painting, literature, photography, theater, dance, film, or other creative human endeavor? Do you agree with the author that art can change the world?

The author compares Francis to Shakespeare's drunks and fools—"the proverbial comic relief." But if Francis was drunk, she argues, "it was on the riotous love of God," and if he was a fool, it was for the sake of the gospel and the need to be utterly transformed by it. Can you think of someone in history or in our world today—or in your life—who is willing to be a fool for God or for what they believe in? How do people respond to this person? What about him or her do you admire?

When the author's fractured navicular heals, she is ecstatic about her newfound freedom to actively engage life again, but she confesses a fear: "What if all I've learned has been in vain?" Sometimes we spend our difficult seasons looking forward to being through with them, only to realize on the other side that there was a sweetness and clarity in learning to trust, rest, and find peace. Have you experienced this sweetness and clarity during a troubled season of your life? Did it disappear when that season passed, or were you able to hold on to it when life returned to "normal"?

Exercises for Spiritual Growth

In the spirit of Saint Francis, the author aspires to give up certain worldly goods and attitudes, among them her "solemn right to complain" (p. 24). Most of us complain more than we realize—about the weather, our circumstances, or another person's behavior. Consider setting aside a day, a few days, or a week—maybe longer—to fast from complaining. If you accidentally complain, forgive yourself, recommit to your fast, and continue. When you feel tempted to complain, see that as an opportunity for gratitude for the many things that have gone well for you. At the end of your fast, journal what you found hard or surprising about the experience—or tell someone you trust about the experience and what you learned.

On the one hand, our possessions are the things we own, but on the other hand, in many ways our possessions end up owning us. The author says that defending her possessions against "dust, oil stains, odors, grime" is a game she plays but almost never wins (p. 39). What if our most prized "possessions" were not in fact material things, but, like Francis's, "a dream and a song." List ten material possessions you own that require significant time, maintenance, or resources. Then list ten immaterial "possessions" that mean something to you—a friendship, a hobby, a ritual, a dream, a place you enjoy visiting. Looking at these two lists, how do they make you feel? What do they say about what you really value?

In one of her letters, the author describes rising before dawn to watch the sunrise, only to discover that the sky is cloudy. But then she witnesses the sun pass directly over a small hole in the clouds, briefly flooding the field with light. She asks Francis, "Was the miracle the way the sun cut past that perfect cleft, or that I was there to see?" (p. 60). How many miracles do we miss because we don't notice them, or because we simply fail to see them as miracles? Take ten slips of paper and write on each a miracle that has happened in your life during the past five years—large or small—and place the slips in a jar. Label the jar "miracles." Decorate it if you feel so inclined, and put it in a visible place. Over the course of a month, add to the jar as you witness new miracles. At the end of the month, review the contents of the jar and take time to be thankful.

In modern life, we tend to rely heavily on electronic communication, and letters have become rare. Yet we miss out on something when we type a text, send an email, or make a social media post. These forms of communication are less personal, and they tend not to carry our hearts or ideas with the richness that a letter can. Think about three people you would like to communicate with on a more engaged level and consider writing each a letter over the coming week. Don't worry if you don't have a "reason" to write these letters. Let sitting down to write a letter be its own reason. If it feels more special, write your letters on nice stationery or a card and use a favorite pen, but don't let not having the right "props" get in the way. A piece of lined notebook paper and a #2 pencil will do!

A journal entry can take many forms, so why not a letter, and why not, more specifically, a letter to God? Start a journal, and each day of the coming week, begin or end your day by writing a letter to God. Tell him about your day, your concerns, your blessings, your fears, your gratitude. When you sit down to write, write freely, and don't take your pen off the page until you are done. As you journal in this way, you may find that your letters are becoming prayers. At the end of the week, read through your letter-prayers. What have you learned about yourself from this exercise? In what ways have you become closer to God?

Acknowledgments

In addition to those thanked in the dedication, I would like to extend deep gratitude to my editors at Eerdmans: Lil Copan, whose enthusiasm for this project has been unwavering, and Mary Hietbrink, whose eye for detail helped make the letters sing. Thanks also go to Rachel Bomberger for lending *Larks* her publicity expertise, to Kevin van der Leek for his delightful cover, and to Meg Schmidt for her charming design of the book's interior. The summer I broke my foot, two neighbors, Angela Gale and Barbara Pitfido, graciously did the entirety of my grocery shopping: they quite literally made this book possible, and for this I am exceedingly obliged. I am also exceedingly obliged to the poetry editors of *Sojourners Magazine* and *Pilgrim: A Journal of Catholic Experience* for publishing earlier versions of individual letters to St. Francis in print and online respectively, and to Sarah Arthur, who included several of the letters in her soul-nourishing devotional, *Between Midnight and Dawn: A Literary Guide to Prayer for Lent, Holy Week, and Eastertide* (Paraclete Press, 2016). Finally, I am profoundly indebted to my parents, John and Diana Carroll, whose belief in the educational value of travel landed our family in Europe for the better part of a year when I was ten. Our visit to Assisi planted a seed of wonder, of which this book is the fruit.